Totally WACKY FACTS ABOUT SPACE

EMMA CARLSON BERNE

CAPSTONE PRESS
a capstone imprint

THE UNIVERSE ISN'T DONE GROWING — IT'S STILL EXPANDING OUTWARD IN EVERY DIRECTION.

No one has figured out how big the UNIVERSE is.

The universe has no end, no edges, and no boundaries.

Stars move at 2 million miles (3.2 million kilometers) per hour as the universe EXPANDS.

MANY PEOPLE BELIEVE THAT THE UNIVERSE EXPLODED INTO EXISTENCE DURING THE BIG BANG.

Before the **Big Bang,** the entire universe was the size of a **PEBBLE.**

The universe expanded from a tiny mass in a **TRILLION-TRILLIONTH OF A SECOND.**

Before the Big Bang, there was NO SPACE and NO TIME.

You can still see the light from the Big Bang— it's called **COSMIC MICROWAVE RADIATION.**

cosmic microwave radiation as seen from a European Space Agency spacecraft

Your body is made up of matter from exploded stars in space.

Almost every atom in everything on Earth came from the BIG BANG or EXPLODED, DYING STARS.

SOME GALAXIES LOOK LIKE SPIRALS, SOME LIKE FLAT BALLS, AND SOME HAVE NO PARTICULAR SHAPE.

You can see galaxies 2 million light-years away with the naked eye.

Some stars are as old as the universe itself—
13.8 billion years.

When a star is created, its temperature is 27 million° F (15 million° C).

Stars shine with their own light, but planets shine with reflected light from the Sun.

Mars in Earth's night sky

Stars twinkle because of **EARTH'S** churning atmosphere.

The light from stars has traveled **TRILLIONS OF MILES** (trillions of km) to reach YOUR EYES.

EVERY STAR YOU SEE IS BIGGER THAN THE SUN. THE SUN LOOKS LARGE BECAUSE IT'S CLOSE TO EARTH.

The NORTH STAR rotates in a little circle every day.

THE PISTOL STAR, 25,000 LIGHT-YEARS FROM EARTH, IS AS BRIGHT AS 10 MILLION SUNS.

THERE ARE ABOUT A SEPTILLION STARS IN THE UNIVERSE—THAT'S 10 FOLLOWED BY 24 ZEROS!

When a huge star collapses, a **BLACK HOLE** is created.

The gravity inside a black hole is so strong, even LIGHT can't escape from it.

IF YOU WERE IN A BLACK HOLE, YOUR BODY WOULD STRETCH OUT LIKE A LONG PIECE OF SPAGHETTI.

Supernovas are giant explosions from the death of GIANT STARS.

WHEN A SUPERNOVA EXPLODES, IT CAN OUTSHINE AN ENTIRE GALAXY.

In the Milky Way, supernova explosions happen about once every >50 YEARS.<

In 1006 the **brightest star** explosion was recorded. It was so bright, people could have read at **midnight by its light.**

You can see light from star explosions that happened hundreds of years ago.

If our solar system were the size of a QUARTER,

the Milky Way would be the size of NORTH AMERICA.

THE MILKY WAY IS PACKED WITH ABOUT 100 BILLION STARS.

The **biggest star** in the Milky Way is 1,500 times bigger than the SUN.

The Sun makes as much energy as 100 billion tons (91 billion metric tons) of dynamite exploding EVERY SECOND!

The Sun's core scorches at a whopping 27 million°F (15 million°C)!

An airplane from Earth would take 26 years to reach the Sun!

Sunlight takes **three minutes** to reach Mercury, but more than **five hours** to reach Pluto.

Mercury

Pluto

The surface of the Sun burps and boils like a pot of **OATMEAL.**

SOLAR FLARES SHOOT THOUSANDS OF MILES (THOUSANDS OF KM) INTO SPACE.

If the Sun were the size of a **BASKETBALL**, Earth would be the **HEAD OF A PIN.**

LIFE ON EARTH WOULDN'T EXIST IF THE SUN WERE ANY LARGER OR SMALLER.

WHEN THE SUN FINALLY DIES, IT WILL BE CRUSHED DOWN TO THE SIZE OF EARTH.

AS THE SUN GETS OLDER, IT GETS HOTTER.

The Sun's "gas tank" is about half full—it has burned through about

HALF

E   F

its lifespan.

A 100-pound (45-kg) person would weigh more than 2,700 pounds (1,225 kg) on the Sun.

The Sun's GRAVITY keeps Earth from floating off into space.

DURING A LUNAR ECLIPSE, THE MOON TURNS A COPPER COLOR.

Daylight looks like TWILIGHT during a solar eclipse.

The longest total solar eclipse lasted more than **7 minutes**.

The temperature on Earth can plunge **20°F (11°C)** during a total solar eclipse.

There are **two** solar eclipses per year somewhere on Earth.

LONG AGO SOME CHINESE PEOPLE BELIEVED THAT A DOG BITING THE MOON HAD CAUSED A LUNAR ECLIPSE.

Some people used to think an ECLIPSE meant something **BAD** was going to happen.

THE ANCIENT INCA BELIEVED THAT A LUNAR ECLIPSE WAS CAUSED BY A JAGUAR ATTACKING THE MOON.

THE MOON? I'd rather track down that deer!

Scientists recently found a planet that drifts by itself in space, instead of orbiting a sun.

A REQUIREMENT TO BE A PLANET? YOU HAVE TO BE ALMOST COMPLETELY ROUND.

There are eight planets that orbit the Sun:

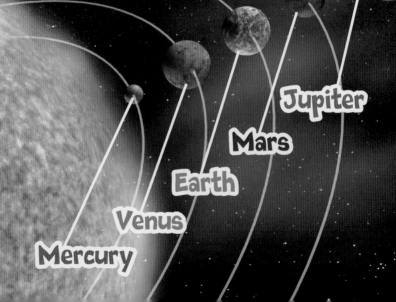

Jupiter

Mars

Earth

Venus

Mercury

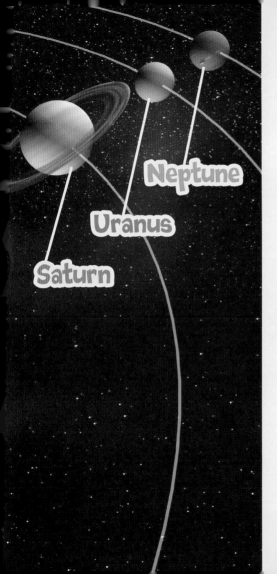

Saturn

Uranus

Neptune

YOU CAN SEE ALL OF THE PLANETS, EXCEPT NEPTUNE, IN THE NIGHT SKY WITHOUT A TELESCOPE.

Mercury's temperature can change 1,090°F (605°C) between night and day.

THE TEMPERATURE ON VENUS IS HOT ENOUGH TO MELT LEAD.

MERCURY HAS NO WIND, WATER, OR ATMOSPHERE, WHICH MEANS IT ALSO HAS NO WEATHER.

From Mercury, the Sun looks three times larger than it does on Earth.

Even though it's closest to the Sun, Mercury is not the hottest planet.

From some parts of Mercury, the Sun appears to get larger as it rises and to shrink as it sets.

The stars move across the sky **THREE TIMES AS FAST** on Mercury as on Earth.

SOME CLIFFS ON MERCURY ARE 1 MILE (1.6 KM) HIGH.

Mercury's surface looks much like our moon's.

ONE CRATER ON MERCURY IS LONGER THAN THE STATE OF CALIFORNIA!

Look carefully! You can see Venus in the sky during the DAY.

Venus is called Earth's sister planet—they are almost the SAME SIZE.

243 Earth days=
1 day on Venus

WHEN COMPARED TO THE OTHER PLANETS, VENUS ROTATES **BACKWARD.**

"SNOW" ON VENUS IS MADE OF METAL.

Venus probably was full of water once, but it has since all BOILED AWAY.

It rains ACID on Venus.

On VENUS the air pressure is so heavy, it would **CRUSH** a person.

EARTH ROTATES EVERY 23 HOURS, 56 MINUTES, AND 4 SECONDS— NOT EVERY 24 HOURS.

EARTH'S SPIN HAS SLOWED DOWN 1.4 THOUSANDTHS OF A SECOND IN THE LAST 100 YEARS.

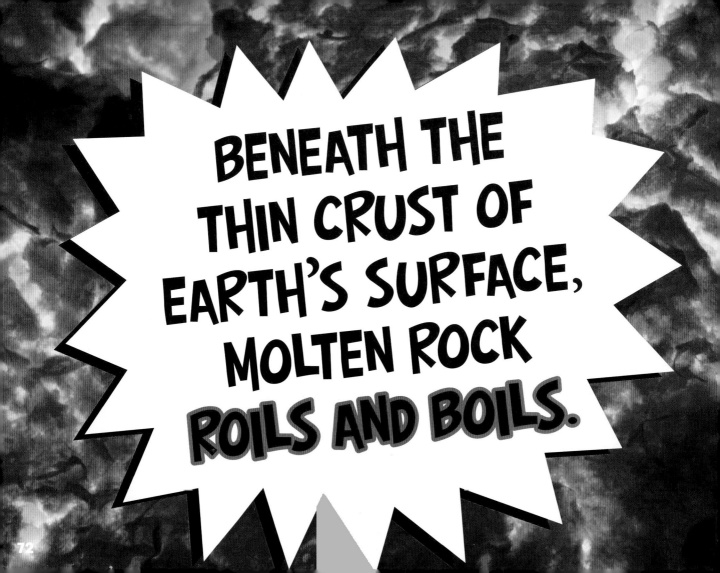

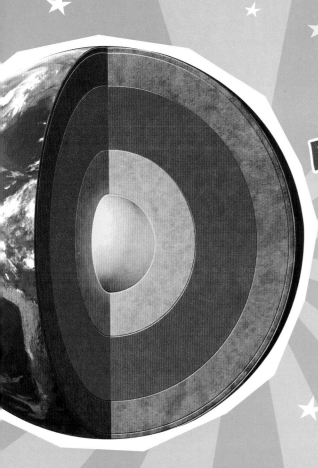

Earth's inner iron core is 9,000 to 13,000° F (4,982 to 7,204° C)!

If you're sending a letter, try writing your FULL address.

Main Street, United States,
Earth, the Solar System,
Orion Arm, the Milky Way,
the Local Group, the Virgo Supercluster,
THE UNIVERSE

Don't forget a stamp!

THE THINNEST PART OF EARTH'S CORE—THE CRUST—CONTAINS ALL THE KNOWN LIFE IN THE UNIVERSE.

MOST OF MARS IS RED-COLORED, BUT THERE ARE PATCHES OF GREEN SOIL. SCIENTISTS DON'T KNOW WHY.

The soil on Mars is RED because it's full of RUST.

IF YOU WEIGHED **100** POUNDS (45 KG) ON **EARTH**, YOU'D WEIGH ONLY **37** POUNDS (17 KG) ON MARS.

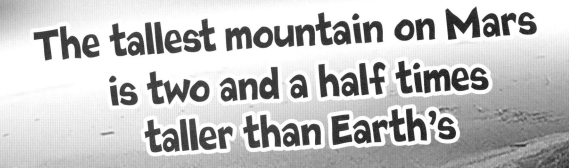

The tallest mountain on Mars is two and a half times taller than Earth's

MOUNT EVEREST.

A HOT, ROCKY DESERT IN CALIFORNIA CALLED DEATH VALLEY IS THE CLOSEST EARTH ENVIRONMENT TO MARS.

Mars has SEASONS like Earth, but they last TWICE AS LONG.

IF YOU SPILLED WATER ON THE SURFACE OF MARS, IT WOULD **FREEZE** AND BOIL AWAY AT THE SAME TIME!

Jupiter's mass is two and a half times larger than that of all the other planets in the solar system COMBINED!

JUPITER IS CALLED THE "GAS GIANT."

Jupiter's day is only 9 hours and 55 minutes long!

ONE YEAR ON JUPITER EQUALS 11.8 EARTH YEARS.

Jupiter's oceans are liquid hydrogen.

HUMANS COULD NEVER LIVE ON JUPITER BECAUSE IT IS COVERED IN CLOUDS OF **POISONOUS GAS.**

JUPITER'S AIR PRESSURE

is so strong it can crush metal as if it were

CARDBOARD.

JUPITER HAS A LARGE SPOT CALLED "THE GREAT RED SPOT."

People have seen the Great Red Spot from Earth since at least **1831**, but possibly since **1665!**

The Great Red Spot is a gigantic, swirling storm that is larger than Earth.

THE GREAT RED SPOT IS SHRINKING.

Saturn rotates ~~~~~~~
10 hours and 34 minutes.

ITS FAST ROTATION MAKES SATURN THE FLATTEST PLANET.

The clouds on Saturn are made of poisonous **AMMONIA ICE CRYSTALS.**

Saturn's windstorms reach 1,000 miles (1,609 km) per hour—twice as fast as an airplane travels.

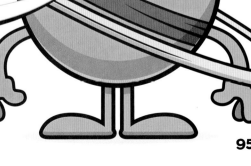

THE RINGS ON SATURN ARE MADE OF CHUNKS OF ICE AND ROCK.

Saturn's rings are 186,000 miles (300,000 km) around, but only ½ mile (0.8 km) thick.

The chunks of ice in Saturn's rings can be as small as a grain of sand or as big as a house.

Uranus is so far away from Earth, it would take about 9 YEARS to get there in a spacecraft!

URANUS IS CALLED THE "ICE GIANT" BECAUSE IT'S MADE UP OF ICE AND ROCK.

Saturn isn't the only planet with rings— Uranus has them too!

Uranus was the first planet anyone discovered with a TELESCOPE.

Uranus may have been hit by two **MASSIVE OBJECTS**, tilting the planet on its side.

BECAUSE OF ITS TILT, URANUS ROLLS LIKE A BARREL ON ITS SIDE.

Uranus takes 84 Earth years to go around the Sun one time.

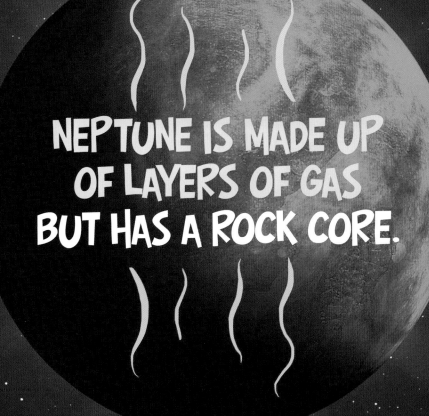

NEPTUNE IS MADE UP OF LAYERS OF GAS BUT HAS A ROCK CORE.

One year on Neptune is nearly 165 Earth years.

BRRR!
THE AVERAGE TEMPERATURE ON NEPTUNE IS -373°F (-225°C).

WINDS WHIP
AROUND ON NEPTUNE AT 1,200 MILES (1,931 KM) PER HOUR.

Scientists think there might be an ocean of **liquid diamond** on Neptune's surface.

The dwarf planet **Pluto** was considered a planet until **2006.**

Pluto is so cold that the air there can freeze and fall like snow.

DWARF PLANETS ARE SMALLER THAN EARTH'S MOON.

WONDERING HOW ALL OF

From smallest to largest, the planets are: Mercury, Mars, Venus, Earth, Neptune, Uranus, Saturn, and Jupiter.

THESE PLANETS COMPARE?

Comets are giant dirty snowballs.

Our solar system is packed with up to 1 trillion comets.

Sometimes a comet's tail is actually in front.

Some comets are famous. **HALLEY'S COMET** even has a name!

SMALL ASTEROIDS AND METEORITES HIT EARTH ALL THE TIME.

Some scientists think an ASTEROID crashed into Earth 65 million years ago and killed all the DINOSAURS.

EARTH'S MOON IS NOT EXACTLY ROUND. IT'S ACTUALLY

EGG-SHAPED.

The surface of Earth's Moon feels like **DAMP BEACH SAND.**

A huge air hockey-like floor helps astronauts learn to move heavy objects in space.

Astronauts train
for space walks
in a giant
SWIMMING POOL.

WANT TO BE AN ASTRONAUT?
FIRST YOU HAVE TO LOG
1,000 HOURS
FLYING JETS!

What does it feel like to float in space? Try riding NASA's VOMIT COMET!

It flies to 34,000 feet (10,363 m), then nosedives to 10,000 feet (3,048 m).

You can live for about 30 seconds in outer space without a space suit of any kind.

Astronaut gloves have heaters inside.

Space suit pants have handles to help pull them on.

On Earth a space suit weighs 280 pounds (127 kilograms) and takes 45 minutes to put on.

Heart muscles can weaken after more than seven days in space.

Long spaceflights give astronauts blurry vision.

SPACE CAN MAKE YOUR HEAD SWELL!

While orbiting Earth, astronauts see a sunset or sunrise every 45 MINUTES.

Some say space smells like meat and metals. Others say it smells like raspberries!

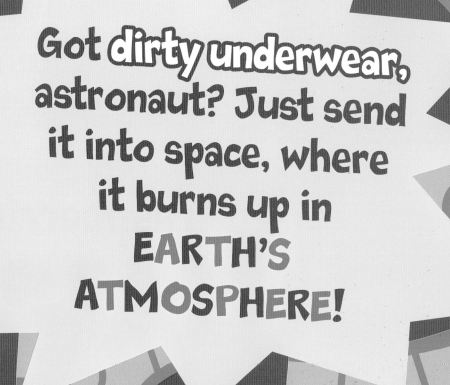

Got **dirty underwear,** astronaut? Just send it into space, where it burns up in EARTH'S ATMOSPHERE!

Astronauts wear special cooling underwear.

129

If an astronaut pukes in space, it floats in LITTLE GLOBS!

131

Astronauts wear adult diapers!

DURING AN EARLY MISSION, AN ASTRONAUT HAD TO WEAR RUBBER PANTS TO POOP IN.

Pants that draw blood to the legs make an astronaut's heart work HARDER IN SPACE.

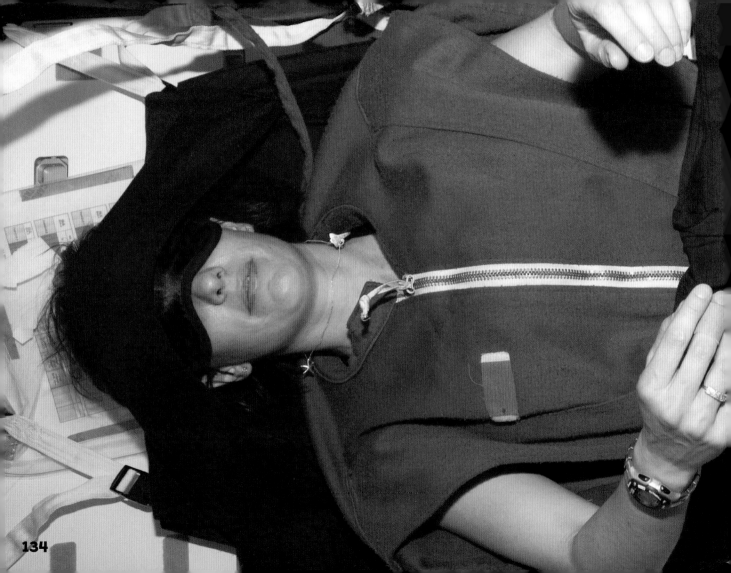

An astronaut straps herself down with **VELCRO** to keep from floating around during sleep.

DURING A **ROCKET LAUNCH,** G-FORCES MAKE YOUR BODY FEEL **FOUR TIMES HEAVIER.**

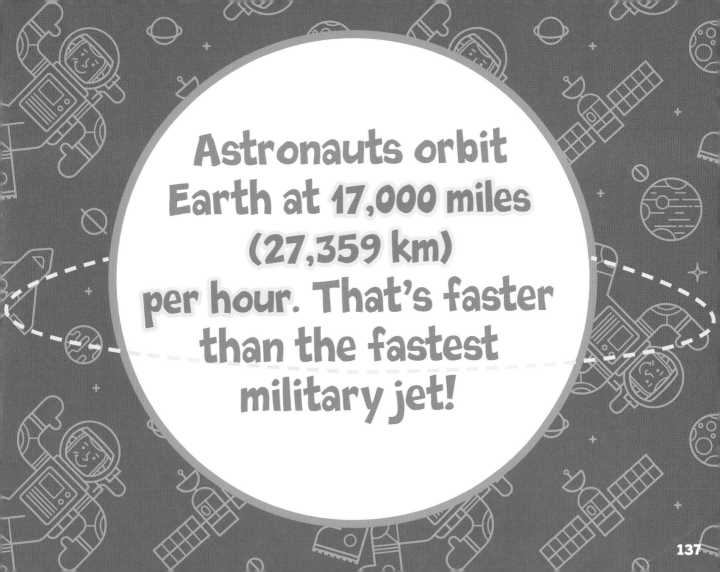

Astronauts orbit Earth at 17,000 miles (27,359 km) per hour. That's faster than the fastest military jet!

Weightlessness in space allows an astronaut to lift really heavy things.

MISSION CONTROL

SOMETIMES WAKES UP ASTRONAUTS BY BLASTING THEIR FAVORITE SONGS.

Astronauts in space **exercise** every day to keep their bodies from weakening.

ASTRONAUTS USED TO EAT FOOD FROM TOOTHPASTE-LIKE TUBES.

The first astronauts in space ate dried food that was **cubed** or made into a **powder.**

To prepare for a space walk, an astronaut spends **four hours** breathing oxygen in a **special chamber.**

A **robotic arm** carries space-walking astronauts from place to place.

During a space walk, the temperature outside can be as high as **250°F (121°C)** or as low as **-250°F (-157°C)**.

AFTER RETURNING FROM SPACE, AN ASTRONAUT MAY FALL OVER WHEN WALKING.

Astronauts who spend a lot of time in space can have BONE LOSS.

Today the International Space Station (ISS) is as large as a U.S. football field!

250 MILES (402 KM): THE DISTANCE FROM EARTH TO THE ISS

The first two parts of the ISS were launched into space in 1998.

Astronauts have an oven and a toaster onboard the ISS, but no refrigerator or microwave.

THE ISS HAS TWO BATHROOMS AND A GYM.

A six-bedroom house has as much living space as the ISS.

IN SPACE, SODA POP BUBBLES SEPARATE FROM THE SODA.

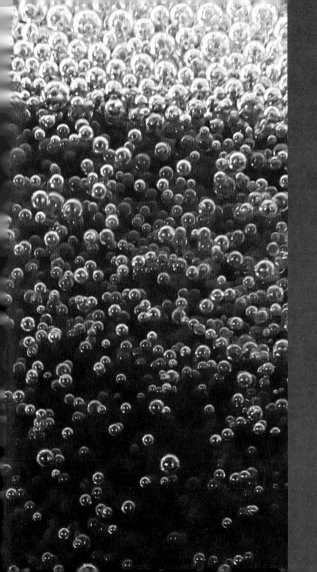

Astronauts use liquid salt because floating salt crystals could get stuck in vents.

Toilets in space work like giant vacuum cleaners.

ON THE ISS PEE IS PURIFIED AND TURNED INTO DRINKING WATER.

On the ISS astronauts wash their hair with a pouch of hot water and rinseless shampoo.

ASTRONAUTS IN SPACE CLEAN THEMSELVES WITH WIPES AND TOWELS.

Dogs, mice, rabbits, turtles, jellyfish, insects, spiders, and fish have all traveled into SPACE.

MORE THAN
2,000 ANIMALS
WENT ON ONE
SPACE MISSION
IN 1998.

In 1957 a Russian dog named Laika was the first live being to orbit EARTH.

A satellite has to zoom along at about **17,500 miles (28,164 km) per hour** to stay in orbit.

The Soviet Union launched the first artificial satellite, *Sputnik 1*, in 1957. It was the size of a BEACH BALL.

A Russian named Yuri Gagarin was the first human to orbit Earth in 1961.

About one month later, Alan Shepard Jr. became the first American in space.

IN 1968 THE EUROPEAN SPACE RESEARCH ORGANIZATION LAUNCHED THE FIRST EUROPEAN SATELLITE INTO SPACE.

In 1962 John Glenn sped around Earth three times. He was the first American to ORBIT EARTH.

ON GLENN'S RETURN TO EARTH, HIS SPACE CAPSULE NEARLY **BURNED UP.**

Astronaut John Glenn was 77 years old during his last space mission.

SCIENTISTS ONCE THOUGHT MOON DUST WOULD SWALLOW A SPACECRAFT TRYING TO LAND ON THE MOON.

THE *RANGER* SPACECRAFT WERE DESIGNED TO ZOOM TOWARD THE MOON, TAKE A BUNCH OF PICTURES, AND THEN CRASH.

The Apollo 11 astronauts practiced moon walking at the GRAND CANYON.

NEIL ARMSTRONG

MICHAEL COLLINS

BUZZ ALDRIN

ON JULY 20, 1969, APOLLO 11 ASTRONAUTS NEIL ARMSTRONG AND BUZZ ALDRIN LANDED ON THE MOON.

168

THE APOLLO 11 ASTRONAUTS TRAVELED 240,000 MILES (386,243 KM) IN 76 HOURS.

ARMSTRONG AND ALDRIN SPOKE TO PRESIDENT NIXON ON THE PHONE FROM THE MOON.

When Armstrong and Aldrin landed on the moon, they had only **20–40 seconds** of fuel left in the lunar module.

Aldrin said walking on the moon was like walking on a trampoline, without bounciness.

THE APOLLO 11 ASTRONAUTS SAVED THEIR LIVES WITH A PEN WHEN A SPACECRAFT SWITCH BROKE OFF.

An American flag that Armstrong and Aldrin had planted on the moon fell over as the lunar module blasted off.

174

IN AN EMERGENCY APOLLO 13 ASTRONAUTS MADE CARBON DIOXIDE FILTERS OUT OF CARDBOARD, PLASTIC BAGS, AND DUCT TAPE.

Astronaut Alan Shepard Jr. played GOLF on the MOON.

The first U.S. space station, **Skylab**, orbited Earth from 1973 to 1979.

Skylab was about as long as a 6-story building!

In 1979 *Skylab* crashed into the Indian Ocean, and some parts fell onto land in Western Australia.

In 1977 the United States launched twin spacecraft, *Voyager 1* and *Voyager 2*, into space.

TITAN/CENTAUR

BOTH *VOYAGER 1* AND *VOYAGER 2* TAKE PICTURES SHARP ENOUGH TO READ A NEWSPAPER HEADLINE FROM ½ MILE (0.8 KM) AWAY.

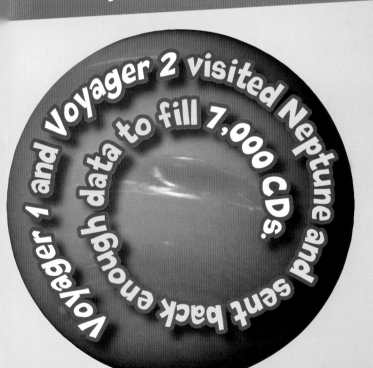

Voyager 1 and Voyager 2 visited Neptune and sent back enough data to fill 1,000 CDs.

VOYAGER 1 has traveled farther from Earth than any other spacecraft.

Just before blasting off into space, astronaut Alan Shepard Jr. told Mission Control that he had to PEE.

In 1980 a European company called Arianespace became the first commercial space transport company.

In 1981 the first U.S. space shuttle, Columbia, launched from Kennedy Space Center, in Florida.

Columbia weighed 178,000 pounds (80,739 kg)—as much as 13 elephants!

THE SHUTTLE'S HEAT SHIELD WAS BUILT USING MORE THAN 30,000 TILES MADE OF SAND.

The space shuttle *Discovery* put on enough miles to go to the moon and back 300 times!

In 1963 Valentina Tereshkova from Russia became the first woman in space.

EILEEN COLLINS BECAME THE FIRST WOMAN TO PILOT A SPACECRAFT WHEN SHE PILOTED THE *DISCOVERY* IN 1995.

NASA retired the space shuttles in 2011, after 30 years of service.

About 400 TREES had to be cut down so the shuttle *Endeavour* could fit through the streets on its trip to the museum.

ENDEAVOUR WAS FLOWN ON TOP OF A JETLINER WHEN IT WENT TO A MUSEUM.

N905NA

The Hubble Space Telescope is as long as a LARGE SCHOOL BUS.

HUBBLE WEIGHS AS MUCH AS TWO ELEPHANTS.

Every hour and a half, Hubble makes one trip around Earth.

191

HUBBLE CAN SEE GALAXIES THAT ARE BILLIONS OF LIGHT-YEARS AWAY.

Hubble can see comet pieces crash into the **atmosphere** above Jupiter.

The Hubble Telescope helped discover dark matter—strange energy that helps the

UNIVERSE EXPAND.

HUBBLE IS THE ONLY TELESCOPE EVER DESIGNED TO BE REPAIRED IN SPACE.

Hubble can see better than ground telescopes, because Earth's atmosphere isn't in the way.

SUNLIGHT POWERS THE HUBBLE TELESCOPE.

THE JAMES WEBB SPACE TELESCOPE (JWST) IS THE NEXT HUBBLE—AND A SORT OF TIME MACHINE.

JWST WILL BE ABLE TO SEE THE FIRST STARS FROM THE BEGINNING OF THE UNIVERSE.

JWST can see the writing on a penny 24 miles (39 km) away.

The JWST can fold up to fit inside a rocket only 16 feet (5 m) wide.

JWST HAS INSTRUMENTS THAT ARE KEPT COLDER THAN -370°F (-223°C) IN ORDER TO OPERATE.

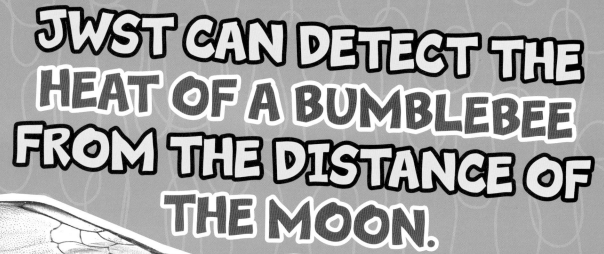

JWST CAN DETECT THE HEAT OF A BUMBLEBEE FROM THE DISTANCE OF THE MOON.

IN 2014 THE EUROPEAN SPACE AGENCY (ESA) SPACECRAFT *ROSETTA* RELEASED A SMALL PROBE THAT LANDED ON A COMET.

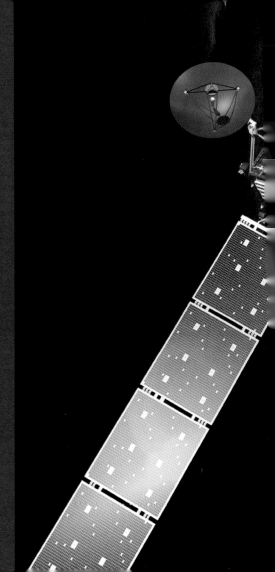

Scientists are tracking 500,000 pieces of space junk orbiting Earth right now.

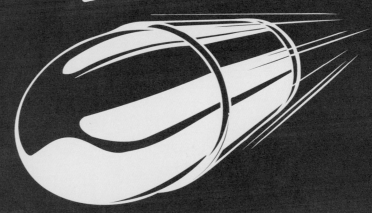

SPACE JUNK MOVES AT 17,500 MILES (28,164 KM) PER HOUR AND CAN ACT LIKE BULLETS.

POOP IS SOME OF THE SPACE JUNK ORBITING EARTH.

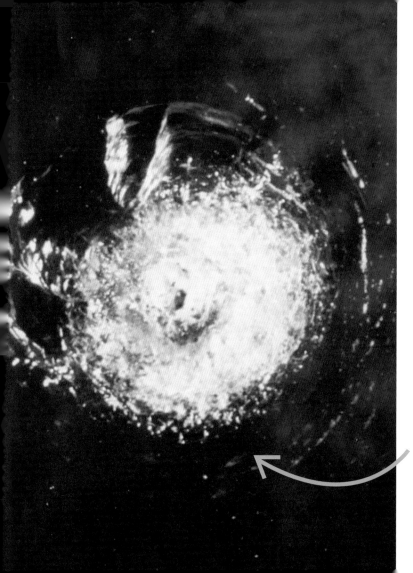

PAINT FLECKS

can move so fast in orbit, that they have cracked spacecraft windows.

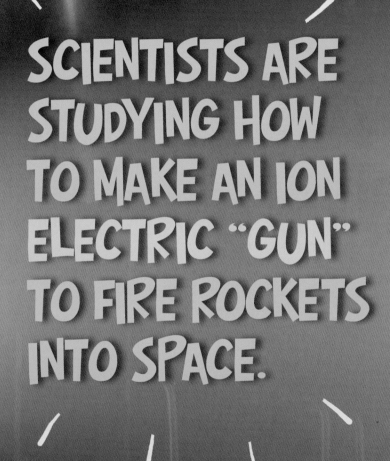

SCIENTISTS ARE STUDYING HOW TO MAKE AN ION ELECTRIC "GUN" TO FIRE ROCKETS INTO SPACE.

Sail-like mirrors that capture sunlight may one day power spacecraft.

NASA's goal is to send astronauts to land on an ASTEROID by 2025.

Astronauts could explore the asteroid to practice for a Mars landing.

THE ROVERS SPIRIT AND OPPORTUNITY HAVE EXPLORED SEVERAL MILES OF MARS.

THE ROVERS WERE SUPPOSED TO RUN FOR ONLY 90 DAYS.

SPIRIT OPERATED FOR 6 YEARS, AND OPPORTUNITY IS STILL RUNNING 10 YEARS LATER.

The Mars rover Curiosity is about as tall as a basketball player.

CURIOSITY HAS A HEAD, ARMS, and LEGS.

Curiosity can take pictures of objects smaller than the width of a **human hair.**

Curiosity takes SELFIES.

215

IN 2005 THE ESA PROBE *HUYGENS* LANDED ON **SATURN'S MOON TITAN.** NO OTHER SPACECRAFT LAUNCHED FROM EARTH HAS LANDED FARTHER AWAY.

In the 19th century, people saw canals on Mars with telescopes.

IN 1965 WE GOT THE FIRST CLOSE LOOK AT MARS FROM A SMALL SPACECRAFT FLYBY.

The first spacecraft on Mars took pictures for **20 seconds** before it went

DARK.

Astronaut Umberto Guidoni became the first European to visit the ISS in 2001.

IN 2001 DENNIS TITO PAID $20 MILLION TO RUSSIAN SPACE OFFICIALS FOR A 10-DAY TRIP TO SPACE!

DENNIS A. TITO
ДЕННИС А. ТИТО

WANT TO TAKE A RIDE TO SPACE?

GALA

Virgin

N339SS

For $250,000 you can sign up for a future seat on a Virgin Galactic spacecraft.

CAN YOU

At almost 438 days, Russian Valeri Polyakov holds the record for the most consecutive days in space.

BEAT THIS?

THE LONGEST SPACE WALK LASTED 8 HOURS AND 56 MINUTES!

The fastest human spaceflight flew at 24,791 miles (39,897 km) per hour!

225

ONLY THE UNITED STATES AND THE FORMER SOVIET UNION HAVE LANDED SPACECRAFT ON MARS.

NASA's *New Horizons* probe conducted a flyby study of Pluto in 2015.

THE PLUTO PROBE TOOK **9 ½ YEARS** TO REACH PLUTO.

IT WAS THE
FASTEST
SPACECRAFT
EVER LAUNCHED.

GOT $100 MILLION? YOU CAN BUY A TRIP AROUND THE **MOON!**

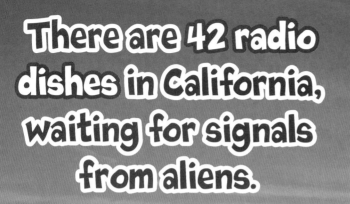

There are 42 radio dishes in California, waiting for signals from aliens.

A signal sent from aliens might take millions of years to reach Earth.

GLOSSARY

artificial—made by people

asteroid—a small rocky object that orbits the sun

atmosphere—the layer of gases that surrounds some planets, dwarf planets, and moons

Big Bang—a sudden event that many scientists say may have caused the beginning of the universe

black hole—invisible region of space with a strong gravitational field

carbon dioxide—an odorless, colorless gas made of carbon and oxygen atoms

comet—a ball of rock and ice that circles the Sun

commercial—to do with buying and selling things

eclipse—when one object in space blocks light and keeps it from shining on another object in space

g-force—the force of gravity on a moving object

galaxy—a large group of stars and planets

gravity—a force that pulls objects together

hydrogen—a colorless gas that is lighter than air and burns easily

International Space Station (ISS)—a place for astronauts to live and work in space

ion—an atom that has an electrical charge

lunar—having to do with a moon

lunar module—a moon vehicle

mass—a body of matter with no particular shape

234

Milky Way—the galaxy in which our Sun is located

molten—melted by heat; lava is molten rock

orbit—to travel around an object in space; an orbit is also the path an object follows while circling an object in space

satellite—an object, either natural or man-made, that orbits a planet

solar—having to do with the Sun

solar flare—gas that shoots out from the Sun's surface

supernova—an exploding star

transport—to move something from one place to another

ABOUT THE AUTHOR

Emma Carlson Berne has written more than a dozen books for children and young adults, including teen romance novels, biographies, and history books. She lives in Cincinnati, Ohio, with her husband, Aaron, her son, Henry, and her dog, Holly.

LOOKING FOR MORE TOTALLY WACKY TRIVIA?

INDEX

Mind Benders are published by Capstone,
1710 Roe Crest Drive, North Mankato, Minnesota 56003
www.capstonepub.com
Editor: Shelly Lyons
Designer: Aruna Rangarajan
Media Researcher: Svetlana Zhurkin
Creative Director: Nathan Gassman
Production Specialist: Lori Barbeau

Library of Congress Cataloging-in-Publication Data
Cataloging-in-publication information is on file with the Library of Congress.
Written by Emma Carlson Berne
ISBN 978-1-4914-6526-4 (paperback)
ISBN 978-1-4914-6536-3 (eBook PDF)

Photo Credits
Alamy: RIA Novosti, cover (bottom left), 159; ESA, 216, ATG Medialab and Rosetta/NavCam, 202—203, DLR/FU Berlin, G. Neukum, 82—83, Planck Collaboration, 7; Getty Images: Sovfoto, 224 (bottom left), SSPL, 218, UIG/Sovfoto, 162; iStockphoto: PeopleImages, cover (bottom right), 8 (bottom); NARA: DoD, 119; NASA, cover (top left), 121, 126, 129, 131, 134—135, 139, 141, 142—143, 146, 152, 153, 163, 164, 168, 170 (front), 173, 174, 177, 179, 180, 181, 183, 184—185, 186, 188—189, 190 (top), 196, 198, 207, 208, 209, 226, Bill Ingalls, 136, 144, CXC/M. Weiss, 22, ESA/HEIC/The Hubble Heritage Team (STScI/AURA), cover (middle right), 8 (top), ESA/J. Hester and A. Loll (Arizona State University), 24, ESA/M.J. Jee and H. Ford (Johns Hopkins University), 192—193, ESA/The Hubble Heritage Team (STScI/AURA), 10, HST Comet Team, 193 (inset), JHUAPL/SwRI, 228—229, Johns Hopkins University Applied Physics Laboratory/Carnegie Institution of Washington, 56—57, 60—61, JPL, 90—91, JPL/Space Science Institute, 85, 92—93, JPL-Caltech, 212, JPL-Caltech/MSSS, 215, MOLA Science Team/O. de Goursac, Adrian Lark, 78—79, N. Walborn and J. Maíz-Apellániz (Space Telescope Science Institute, Baltimore, MD)/R. Barbá (La Plata Observatory, La Plata, Argentina), 13; Newscom: Design Pics/Carson Ganci, 14—15, Reuters/Mikhail Grachyev, 221, Rex, 187, Zuma Press/Mark Greenberg, 222—223; Shutterstock: advent, 171, Ahturner, back cover (left), 125 (front), Aleks Melnik, 132, Alexander Mazurkevich, 172, Alexey Bragin, 28, Anastasia Mazeina, 156, 157, Andrea Danti, 73, Anteromite, 175 (bottom), argus, 55, Asif Islam, 80, AstroStar, 26—27, billdayone, 103, blambca, 148, BortN66, 170 (TV), Byron W. Moore, 106, Christopher Ewing, 72, Christopher Gardiner, 18, Christos Georghiou, 34, Computer Earth, 35, Cory Thoman, 12 (right), 95 (right), Crystal Eye Studio, 227, Designsstock, 32—33, Diana Beato, 167, Eldad Carin, 117, Elena Abramova, 214, Esteban De Armas, 115, Everett Collection, 169, Everett Historical, 112—113, Fisherss, 191 (bottom), Fred Fokkelman, 50—51, Giantrabbit, 9, Givaga, 100, Good Vector, 205, Graphic Compressor, 160, Gyvafoto, 2 (right), Halina Yakushevich, 127, Harvepino, 29, HelenField, 64—65, Hurst Photo, 161, Ian Doktor, 116, Igor Zh., 4, 5 (right), IhorZigor, 200 (right), irin-k, 38 (left), Ivan Nikulin, 232, ivn3da, 104, Jack Ammit, 49, Johan Swanepoel, 204, kakin, 125 (back), Keattikorn, 176, KMW Photography, 21 (bottom), Koshevnyk, 140, kukaruka, 67, La Gorda, 95 (bubbles), lassedesignen, 77, Lisa Yen, 206, Maaike Boot, 128, Marcel Clemens, 101, Marija Piliponyte, 86, Mateusz Gzik, 74, Matthias Pahl, 66 (front), mayakova, 38 (right), Mega Pixel, 89 (bottom), 175 (top), Melica, 224, Memo Angeles, 12 (left), Michelangelus, 39, MisterElements, 225 (bottom right), Mopic, 58, Morphart Creation, 217, Naeblys, 108—109, Nikita Maykov, 30—31, NikoNomad, 76, 147, Olga Danylenko, 5 (left), Orla, 52—53, owncham, 105, Pal Teravagimov, 79 (inset), Palto, 118, Patrick Foto, 16, Paul Fleet, 110—111, 195, Paulo Afonso, 233, Pavel Smilyk, 3, Petros Tsonis, 230—231, Pixel Embargo, 97, Pixsooz, 149, Protasov AN, 201, Q-lieb-in, 199, R G Meier, 44, rangizzz, 124, Rich Koele, 190 (bottom), Richard Peterson, 191 (top), Rob Byron, 71, robodread, 178, Sabphoto, 17, 42, Sebastian Crocker, 89 (top), SergeyDV, 96, 210—211, Shane Maritch, 200 (left), Shirstok, 137, stockphoto mania, back cover (right), 122—123, Tribalium, 224 (bottom right), Triff, 43, Tristan3D, 63, Vadim Sadovski, cover (top right), 102, ValoValo, 98, Vasilis Ververidis, 20, Vladimir Wrangel, 46, Voraorn Ratanakorn, 107, Winai Tepsuttinun, 175 (left), Yayayoyo, 194, Yorik, 150; SOHO (ESA & NASA), 37; SuperStock: Science and Society, 48 (front); Svetlana Zhurkin, 36; Wikimedia: Mike Young, 99

Design Elements by Capstone and Shutterstock

Printed in China.
032015   008869RRDF15